POPULAR SONGS
HAL LEONARD
STUDENT PIANO LIBRARY

Top Piano Ballads

Arranged by Jennifer Watts

T0081609

ISBN 978-1-4950-7574-2

HAL•LEONARD®
7777 W. BLUEMOUND RD. P.O. BOX 13819 MILWAUKEE, WI 53213

Visit Hal Leonard Online at
www.halleonard.com

From the Arranger

Preparing these arrangements was both a reward as well as a challenge. The challenge was making these arrangements playable for the young student, and the reward was producing music that is educational and enjoyable for the student to play. These are beautiful songs, and my hope is that they add joy to your piano playing.

Jennifer Watts

Living in Southern California, Jennifer Watts is a jazz artist as well as a classical pianist. Jennifer received her music degree at California State University, Chico, and currently maintains an independent piano studio in Los Alamitos. She has contributed articles to the *California Music Teacher* magazine on improvisation and accompanying. In addition, she is a pianist and choir accompanist for the Grace Community Church in Seal Beach.

CONTENTS

All of Me

Words and Music by John Stephens
and Toby Gad
Arranged by Jennifer Watts

With feeling (♩ = c. 116)

mp
With pedal
What would I do with - out your smart mouth draw - in' me in and you kick - ing me out? You've got my head spin - nin', no kid - din'. I can't pin you down. What's go - in'
How man - y times do I have to tell you, e - ven when you're cry - ing, you're beau - ti - ful too? The world is beat - ing you down, I'm a - round through ev - er - y mood. You're my

on in that beau - ti - ful mind? ___ I'm on your mag - i - cal mys - ter - y ride. ___
down - fall, you're my muse, ___ my worst dis - trac - tion, my rhy - thm and blues.

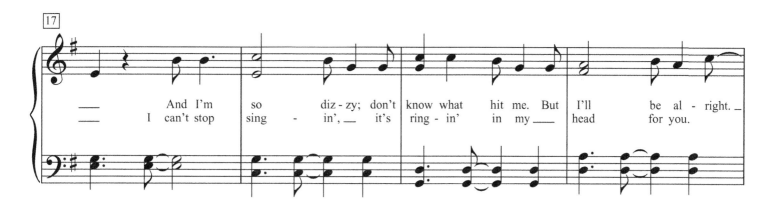

___ And I'm so diz - zy; don't know what hit me. But I'll be al - right. ___
___ I can't stop sing - in', ___ it's ring - in' in my ___ head for you.

___ My head's un - der wa - ter, ___ but I'm ___ breath - ing fine. ___

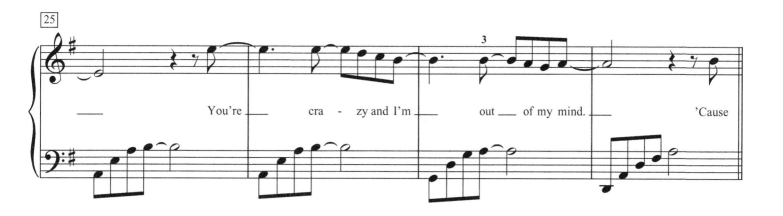

___ You're ___ cra - zy and I'm ___ out ___ of my mind. ___ 'Cause

ning.   E - ven   when   I   lose,   I'm win - ning.   'Cause I give you all ____

____ of me, ____   and you give me all ____

To Coda **1.**   **2.**

____ of you, ____ oh. ____   oh. ____

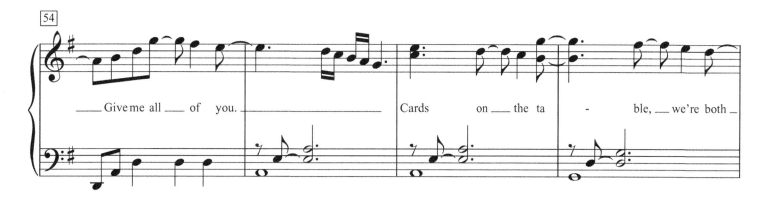

____ Give me all ____ of you. _____   Cards   on ____ the ta - ble, ____ we're both ____

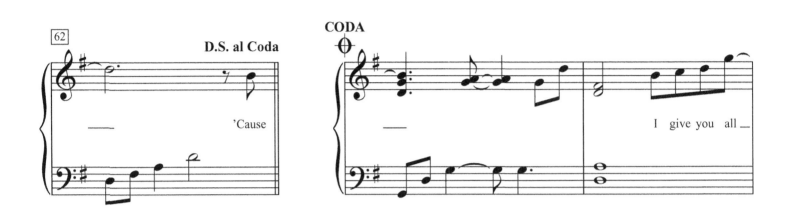

When I Was Your Man

Words and Music by Bruno Mars,
Ari Levine, Philip Lawrence
and Andrew Wyatt
Arranged by Jennifer Watts

-ers _____ and held your hand; ____ should - 've gave you all my hours___

_____ when I had ___ the chance; take ___ you to ev - 'ry par -

- ty, 'cause all ___ you want - ed to do ___ was dance. _____ Now ___ my ba-by's danc-

- ing, ___ but she's danc-ing with an-oth-er man. ___

Al - though it hurts, I'll be the

first to say __ that I was wrong. _____ Oh, I

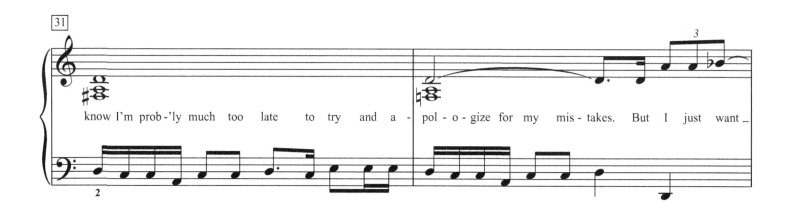

know I'm prob-'ly much too late to try and a - pol - o - gize for my mis - takes. But I just want __

__ you to know, _____ I hope __ he buys __ you

flow- ers, ___ I hope he holds _ your hand, give you all his hours _____ when he has the

chance; take you to ev - 'ry par - ty 'cause I re - mem - ber how much _ you love

to dance; _ do all the things _ I _____ should-'ve done _ when I was your

man. Do all the things I _____ should-'ve done _ when I was your man.

poco rit.

One Call Away

Words and Music by Charlie Puth,
Breyan Isaac, Matt Prime, Justin Franks,
Blake Anthony Carter and Maureen McDonald
Arranged by Jennifer Watts

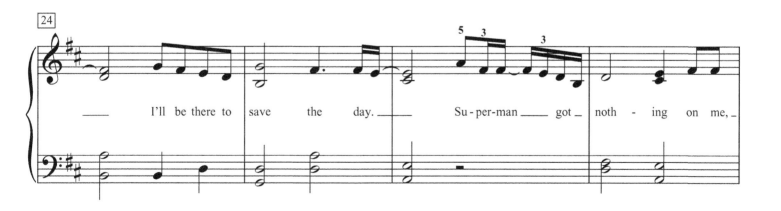

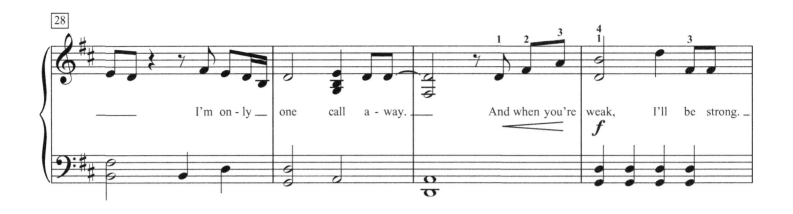

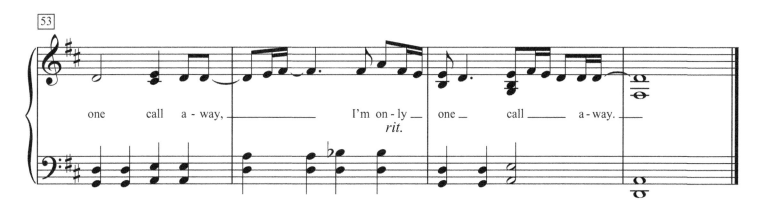

Say Something

Words and Music by Ian Axel,
Chad Vaccarino and Mike Campbell
Arranged by Jennifer Watts

Moderately (♩. = 120)

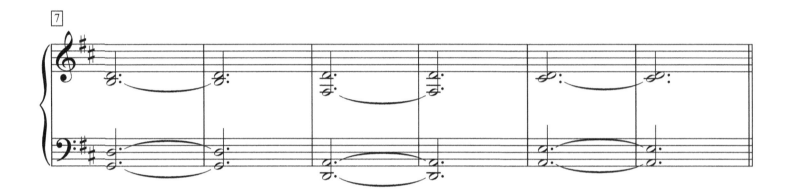

With pedal

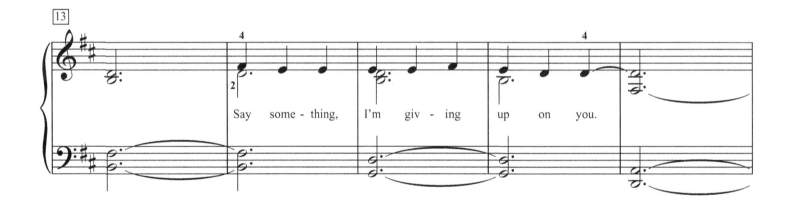

Say some-thing, I'm giv-ing up on you.

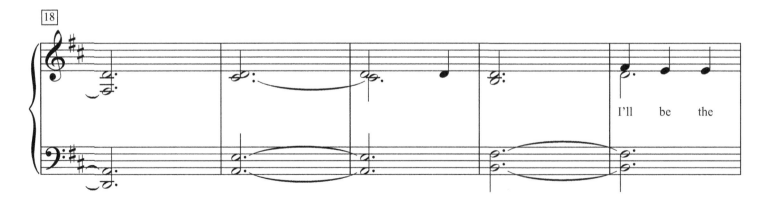

I'll be the

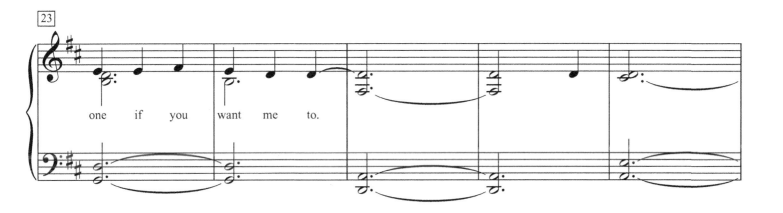

one   if   you   want   me   to.

An - y - where   I   would have   fol - lowed   you. __

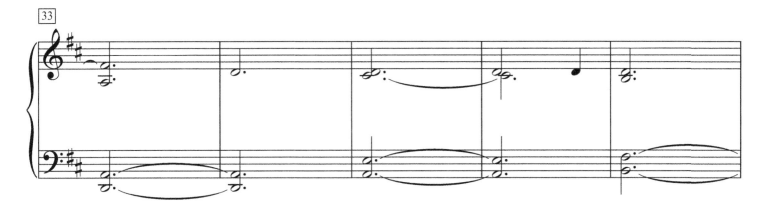

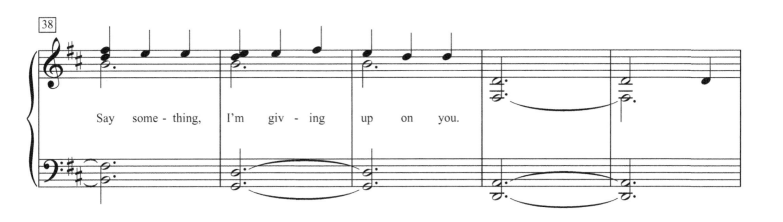

Say   some - thing,   I'm   giv - ing   up   on   you.

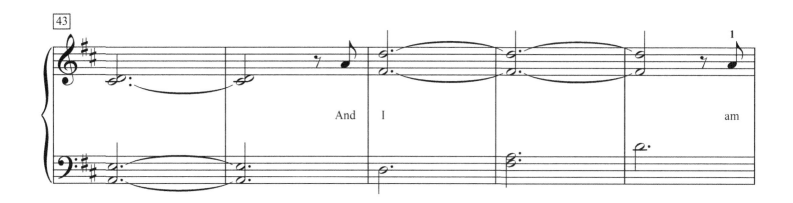

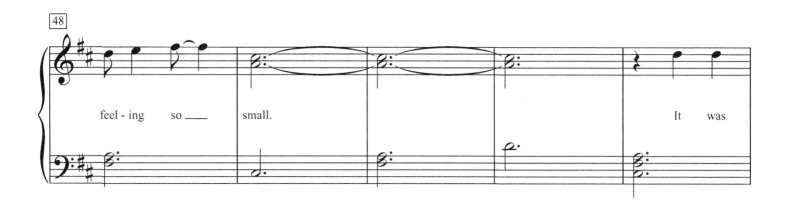

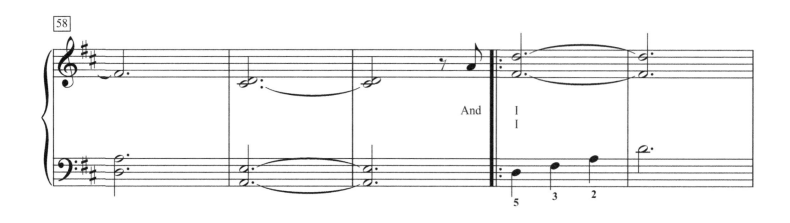

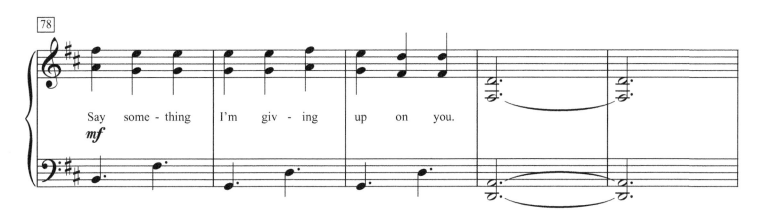

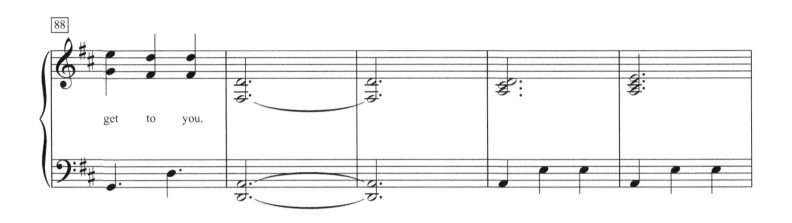

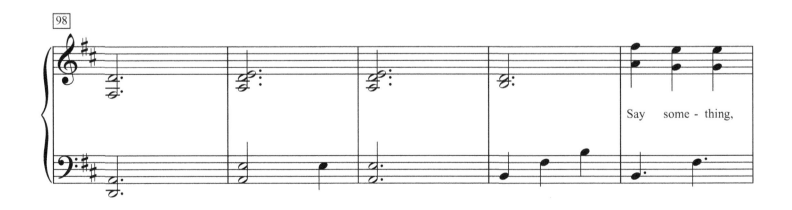

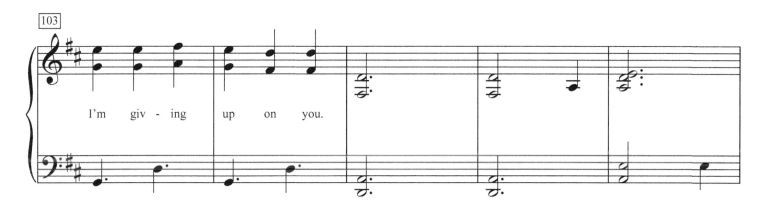

I'm giv - ing up on you.

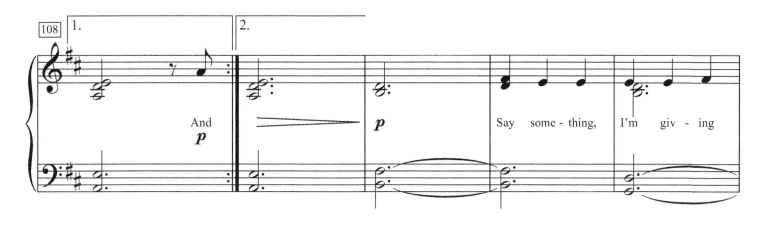

1. And
2.
p
p
Say some - thing, I'm giv - ing

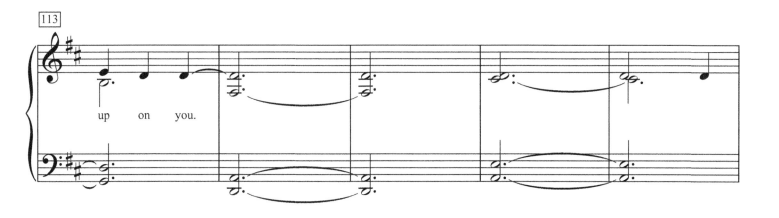

up on you.

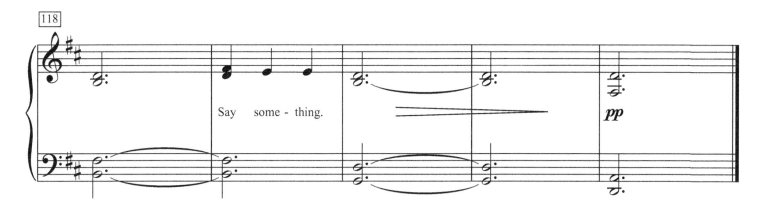

Say some - thing.
pp

See You Again

from FURIOUS 7

Words and Music by Cameron Thomaz,
Charlie Puth, Justin Franks
and Andrew Cedar
Arranged by Jennifer Watts

Soulful (♩ = 80)

mf

With pedal

It's been a long day — with - out you, my friend. — And I'll

tell you all a - bout it when I see you a - gain. — We've come a long way — from

where we be - gan. — Oh, I'll tell you all a - bout it when I see you a - gain, when I

To Coda

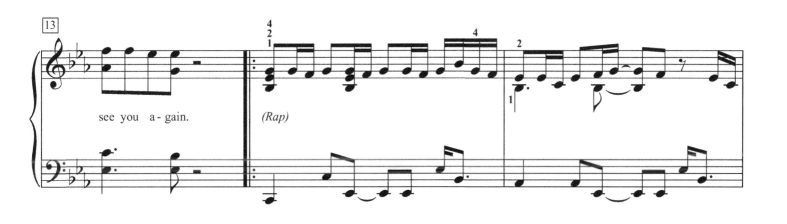

see you a-gain. (Rap)

1.

2.

D.S. al Coda

It's been a

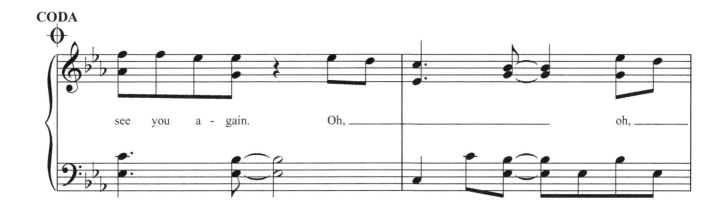

CODA

see you a-gain. Oh, _____ oh,

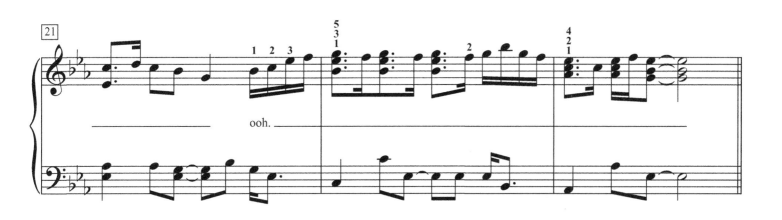

_____ ooh.

(Rap)

So let the

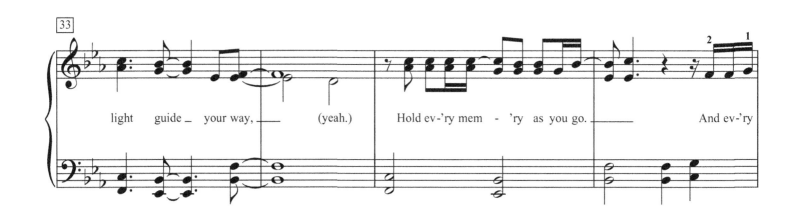

light guide _ your way, ____ (yeah.) Hold ev-'ry mem - 'ry as you go. _____ And ev-'ry

road you take will al - ways ___ lead you home, home. ___ It's been a

long day ___ with - out you, my friend. _ And I'll tell you all a - bout it when I

see you a - gain. _ We've come a long way ___ from where we be - gan. ___ Oh, I'll

tell you all a - bout it when I see you a - gain, ___ when I see you a - gain. ___

7 Years

Words and Music by Lukas Forchhammer,
Morten Ristorp, Stefan Forrest,
David Labrel, Christopher Brown
and Morten Pilegaard
Arranged by Jennifer Watts

Moderately, with a lilt (♩ = 56)

With pedal

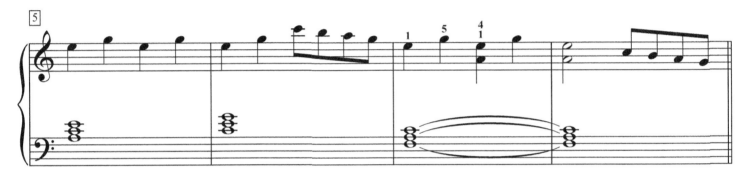

Once I was sev-en years old, my ma-ma told me, "Go make your-self some friends or you'll be lone - ly." —

Once I was sev - en years old.

It was a big, big world, but we thought we were big-ger. Push-ing each oth-er to the

lim-its, we were learn-ing quick-er. By e-lev-en, smok-ing herb and drink-ing burn-ing li-quor.

Nev-er rich so we were out to make that stead-y fig-ure. Once I was e-lev-en years

old, my dad-dy told me, "Go get your-self a wife or you'll be lone-ly." Once I was e-lev-en years old.

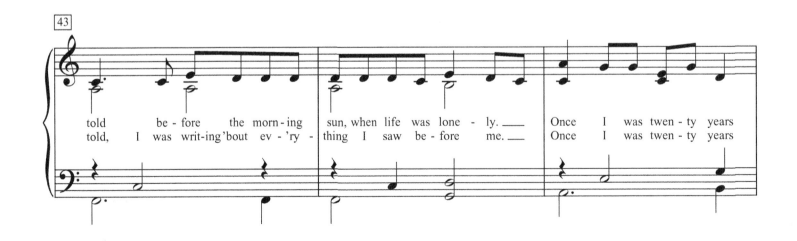

old.
old.

Soon we'll be thir-ty years old. Our songs have been sold, we've trav-elled a-round the world and we're still roam - ing. _

Soon we'll be thir - ty years old.

I'm still learn-ing a-bout life. _ My wom-an brought chil-dren for me so I can sing them all my

songs and I can tell them sto-ries. Most of my boys are with me, some are still out seek-ing glo-ry

and some I had to leave be-hind. My broth-er, I'm still sor-ry. Soon I'll be six-ty years

old. My dad-dy got six-ty-one. Re-mem-ber life and then your life be-comes a bet-ter one.

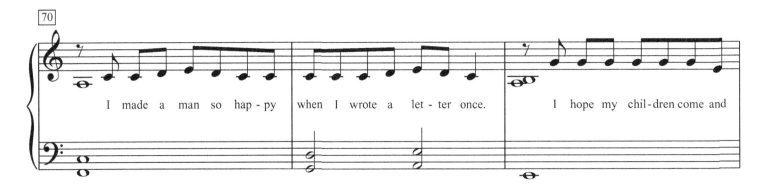

I made a man so hap-py when I wrote a let-ter once. I hope my chil-dren come and

vis-it once or twice a month. Soon I'll be six-ty years old. *cresc.*

Stay with Me

Words and Music by Sam Smith,
James Napier, William Edward Phillips,
Tom Petty and Jeff Lynne
Arranged by Jennifer Watts

I don't want you to leave, will you hold my hand?
But you can lay with me so it does-n't hurt.

Oh, won't you

stay with me? 'Cause you're all I need.

This ain't love, it's clear to see. But, dar-ling,

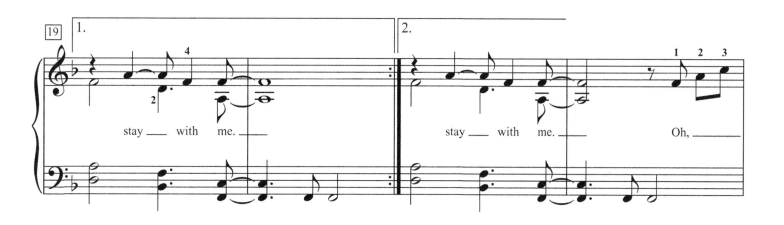

1.
stay with me.

2.
stay with me. Oh,

oh, _____

_____ oh, _____ oh, _____

_____ Oh, won't you stay ____ with me? ____

____ 'Cause you're all ____ I need. ____ This ain't ____

love, it's clear ____ to ____ see. But, dar - ling, ____ stay ____ with me. ____

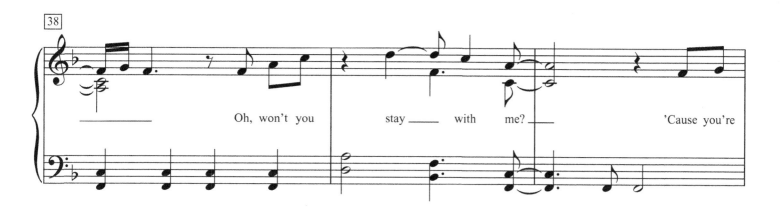

____ Oh, won't you ____ stay ____ with me? ____ 'Cause you're

all ____ I need. ____ This ain't ____ love, it's clear ____ to see. ____

____ But, dar - ling, ____ stay ____ with me. ____

Lost Boy

Words and Music by
Ruth Berhe
Arranged by Jennifer Watts

There was a time when I was a-lone, with no-where to go and no place to call home.

My on-ly friend was The Man in the Moon, and e-ven some-times he would go a-way too.

Then, one night as I closed my eyes, I saw a shad-ow fly-ing high.

He came to me with the sweet-est smile; told me he want-ed to talk for a-while. He said

21 L'istesso (♩. = ♩)

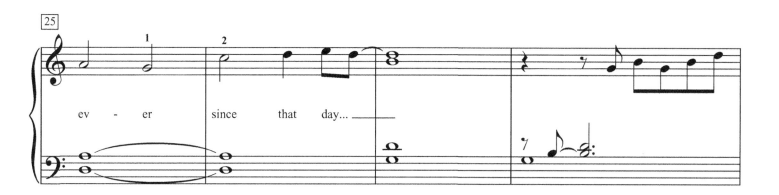

"Pe-ter Pan, that's what they call me. I prom-ise that you'll nev-er be lone-ly." And

ev - er since that day... And

39

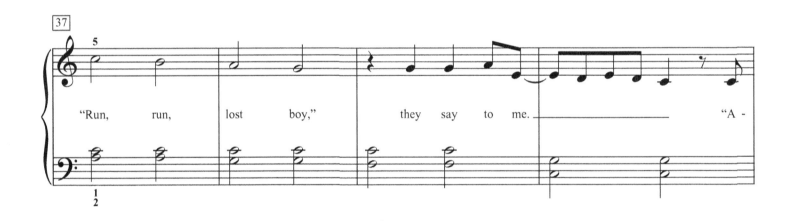

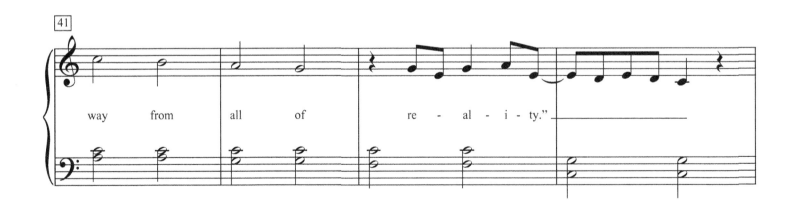

Nev-er-land is home to the lost boys like me; and lost boys like me are free. [He]

sprin-kled me in pix-ie dust and told me to be-lieve, be-lieve in him and be-

lieve in me. "To-geth-er, we will fly a-way in a cloud of green, to your beau-ti-ful

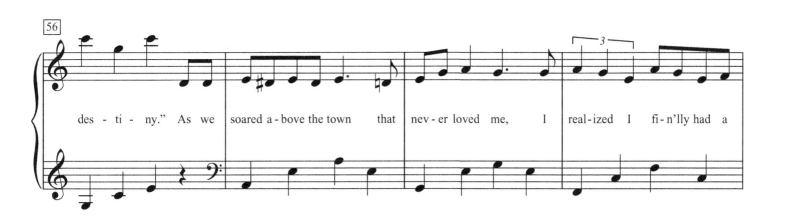

des-ti-ny." As we soared a-bove the town that nev-er loved me, I real-ized I fi-n'lly had a

fam - i - ly.   Soon e-nough, we reached Nev - er - land.   Peace - ful - ly, my feet

hit the sand. And   ev -   er   since   that   day...

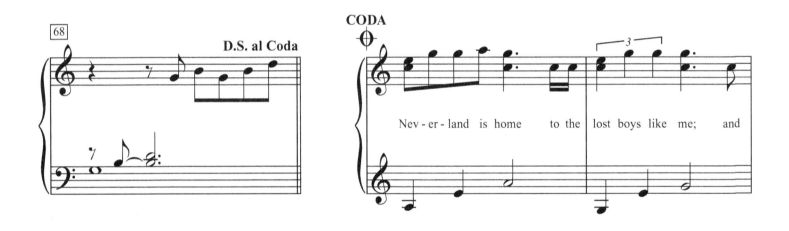

D.S. al Coda

CODA

Nev - er - land is home   to the lost boys like me;   and

lost boys like me are __ free.   Pe - ter Pan, Tin - ker - bell,   Wen - dy Dar - ling,

e - ven Cap - tain Hook: you are my per - fect sto - ry - book. Nev - er - land, I love you so;

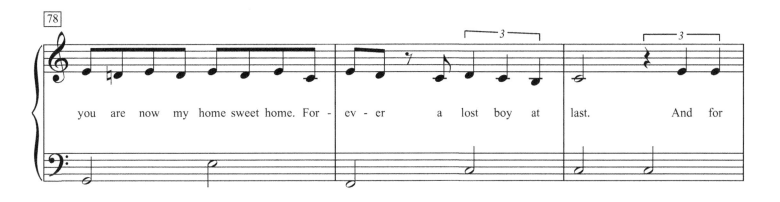

you are now my home sweet home. For - ev - er a lost boy at last. And for

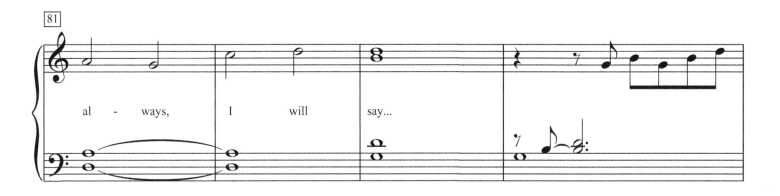

al - ways, I will say...

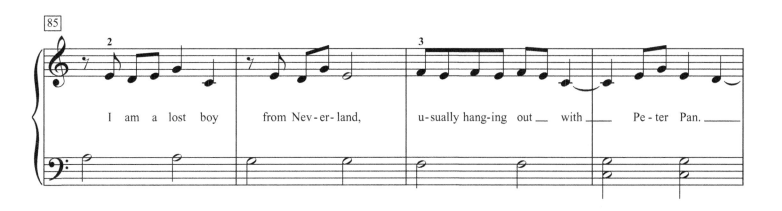

I am a lost boy from Nev - er - land, u-sually hang-ing out __ with __ Pe - ter Pan. ____

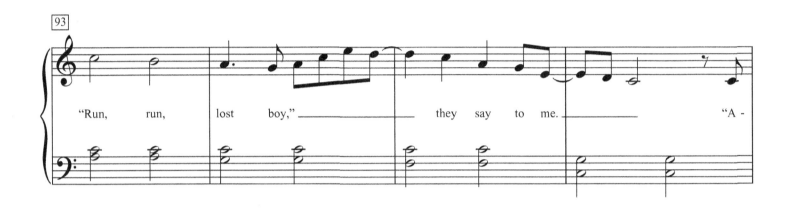

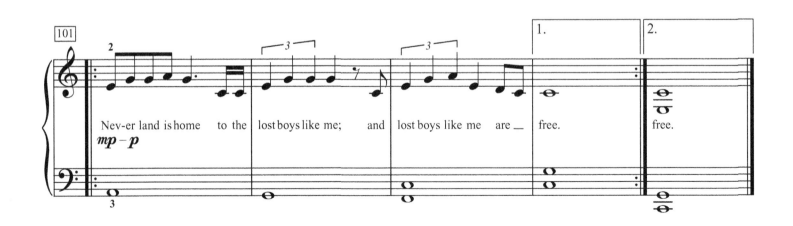

The **Hal Leonard Student Piano Library** has great songs, and you will find all your favorites here: Disney classics, Broadway and movie favorites, and today's top hits. These graded collections are skillfully and imaginatively arranged for students and pianists at every level, from elementary solos with teacher accompaniments to sophisticated piano solos for the advancing pianist.

Adele
arr. Mona Rejino
Correlates with HLSPL Level 5
00159590..............................$12.99

The Beatles
arr. Eugénie Rocherolle
Correlates with HLSPL Level 5
00296649..............................$12.99

Irving Berlin Piano Duos
arr. Don Heitler and Jim Lyke
Correlates with HLSPL Level 5
00296838..............................$14.99

Broadway Favorites
arr. Phillip Keveren
Correlates with HLSPL Level 4
00279192..............................$12.99

Chart Hits
arr. Mona Rejino
Correlates with HLSPL Level 5
00296710..............................$8.99

Christmas at the Piano
arr. Lynda Lybeck-Robinson
Correlates with HLSPL Level 4
00298194..............................$12.99

Christmas Cheer
arr. Phillip Keveren
Correlates with HLSPL Level 4
00296616..............................$8.99

Classic Christmas Favorites
arr. Jennifer & Mike Watts
Correlates with HLSPL Level 5
00129582..............................$9.99

Christmas Time Is Here
arr. Eugénie Rocherolle
Correlates with HLSPL Level 5
00296614..............................$8.99

Classic Joplin Rags
arr. Fred Kern
Correlates with HLSPL Level 5
00296743..............................$9.99

Classical Pop – Lady Gaga Fugue & Other Pop Hits
arr. Giovanni Dettori
Correlates with HLSPL Level 5
00296921..............................$12.99

Contemporary Movie Hits
arr. by Carol Klose, Jennifer Linn and Wendy Stevens
Correlates with HLSPL Level 5
00296780..............................$8.99

Contemporary Pop Hits
arr. Wendy Stevens
Correlates with HLSPL Level 3
00296836..............................$8.99

Cool Pop
arr. Mona Rejino
Correlates with HLSPL Level 5
00360103..............................$12.99

Country Favorites
arr. Mona Rejino
Correlates with HLSPL Level 5
00296861..............................$9.99

Disney Favorites
arr. Phillip Keveren
Correlates with HLSPL Levels 3/4
00296647..............................$10.99

Disney Film Favorites
arr. Mona Rejino
Correlates with HLSPL Level 5
00296809 ....$10.99

Disney Piano Duets
arr. Jennifer & Mike Watts
Correlates with HLSPL Level 5
00113759..............................$13.99

Double Agent! Piano Duets
arr. Jeremy Siskind
Correlates with HLSPL Level 5
00121595..............................$12.99

Easy Christmas Duets
arr. Mona Rejino & Phillip Keveren
Correlates with HLSPL Levels 3/4
00237139..............................$9.99

Easy Disney Duets
arr. Jennifer and Mike Watts
Correlates with HLSPL Level 4
00243727..............................$12.99

Four Hands on Broadway
arr. Fred Kern
Correlates with HLSPL Level 5
00146177..............................$12.99

Frozen Piano Duets
arr. Mona Rejino
Correlates with HLSPL Levels 3/4
00144294..............................$12.99

Hip-Hop for Piano Solo
arr. Logan Evan Thomas
Correlates with HLSPL Level 5
00360950..............................$12.99

Jazz Hits for Piano Duet
arr. Jeremy Siskind
Correlates with HLSPL Level 5
00143248..............................$12.99

Elton John
arr. Carol Klose
Correlates with HLSPL Level 5
00296721..............................$10.99

Joplin Ragtime Duets
arr. Fred Kern
Correlates with HLSPL Level 5
00296771..............................$8.99

Movie Blockbusters
arr. Mona Rejino
Correlates with HLSPL Level 5
00232850..............................$10.99

The Nutcracker Suite
arr. Lynda Lybeck-Robinson
Correlates with HLSPL Levels 3/4
00147906..............................$8.99

Pop Hits for Piano Duet
arr. Jeremy Siskind
Correlates with HLSPL Level 5
00224734..............................$12.99

Sing to the King
arr. Phillip Keveren
Correlates with HLSPL Level 5
00296808..............................$8.99

Smash Hits
arr. Mona Rejino
Correlates with HLSPL Level 5
00284841..............................$10.99

Spooky Halloween Tunes
arr. Fred Kern
Correlates with HLSPL Levels 3/4
00121550..............................$9.99

Today's Hits
arr. Mona Rejino
Correlates with HLSPL Level 5
00296646..............................$9.99

Top Hits
arr. Jennifer and Mike Watts
Correlates with HLSPL Level 5
00296894..............................$10.99

Top Piano Ballads
arr. Jennifer Watts
Correlates with HLSPL Level 5
00197926..............................$10.99

Video Game Hits
arr. Mona Rejino
Correlates with HLSPL Level 4
00300310..............................$12.99

You Raise Me Up
arr. Deborah Brady
Correlates with HLSPL Level 2/3
00296576..............................$7.95

HAL•LEONARD®
7777 W. BLUEMOUND RD. P.O. BOX 13819 MILWAUKEE, WI 53213

Visit our website at www.halleonard.com

Prices, contents and availability subject to change without notice. Prices may vary outside the U.S.

0321
009

This series showcases great original piano music from our **Hal Leonard Student Piano Library** family of composers. Carefully graded for easy selection.

BILL BOYD

JAZZ BITS (AND PIECES)
Early Intermediate Level
00290312 11 Solos......................$7.99

JAZZ DELIGHTS
Intermediate Level
00240435 11 Solos......................$8.99

JAZZ FEST
Intermediate Level
00240436 10 Solos......................$8.99

JAZZ PRELIMS
Early Elementary Level
00290032 12 Solos......................$7.99

JAZZ SKETCHES
Intermediate Level
00220001 8 Solos......................$8.99

JAZZ STARTERS
Elementary Level
00290425 10 Solos......................$8.99

JAZZ STARTERS II
Late Elementary Level
00290434 11 Solos......................$7.99

JAZZ STARTERS III
Late Elementary Level
00290465 12 Solos......................$8.99

THINK JAZZ!
Early Intermediate Level
00290417 Method Book............$12.99

TONY CARAMIA

JAZZ MOODS
Intermediate Level
00296728 8 Solos......................$6.95

SUITE DREAMS
Intermediate Level
00296775 4 Solos......................$6.99

SONDRA CLARK

DAKOTA DAYS
Intermediate Level
00296521 5 Solos......................$6.95

FLORIDA FANTASY SUITE
Intermediate Level
00296766 3 Duets......................$7.95

THREE ODD METERS
Intermediate Level
00296472 3 Duets......................$6.95

MATTHEW EDWARDS

CONCERTO FOR YOUNG PIANISTS
FOR 2 PIANOS, FOUR HANDS
Intermediate Level Book/CD
00296356 3 Movements $19.99

CONCERTO NO. 2 IN G MAJOR
FOR 2 PIANOS, 4 HANDS
Intermediate Level Book/CD
00296670 3 Movements............$17.99

PHILLIP KEVEREN

MOUSE ON A MIRROR
Late Elementary Level
00296361 5 Solos......................$8.99

MUSICAL MOODS
Elementary/Late Elementary Level
00296714 7 Solos......................$6.99

SHIFTY-EYED BLUES
Late Elementary Level
00296374 5 Solos......................$7.99

CAROL KLOSE

THE BEST OF CAROL KLOSE
Early to Late Intermediate Level
00146151 15 Solos...................$12.99

CORAL REEF SUITE
Late Elementary Level
00296354 7 Solos......................$7.50

DESERT SUITE
Intermediate Level
00296667 6 Solos......................$7.99

FANCIFUL WALTZES
Early Intermediate Level
00296473 5 Solos......................$7.95

GARDEN TREASURES
Late Intermediate Level
00296787 5 Solos......................$8.50

ROMANTIC EXPRESSIONS
Intermediate to Late Intermediate Level
00296923 5 Solos......................$8.99

WATERCOLOR MINIATURES
Early Intermediate Level
00296848 7 Solos......................$7.99

JENNIFER LINN

AMERICAN IMPRESSIONS
Intermediate Level
00296471 6 Solos......................$8.99

ANIMALS HAVE FEELINGS TOO
Early Elementary/Elementary Level
00147789 8 Solos......................$8.99

AU CHOCOLAT
Late Elementary/Early Intermediate Level
00298110 7 Solos......................$8.99

CHRISTMAS IMPRESSIONS
Intermediate Level
00296706 8 Solos......................$8.99

JUST PINK
Elementary Level
00296722 9 Solos......................$8.99

LES PETITES IMAGES
Late Elementary Level
00296664 7 Solos......................$8.99

LES PETITES IMPRESSIONS
Intermediate Level
00296355 6 Solos......................$8.99

REFLECTIONS
Late Intermediate Level
00296843 5 Solos......................$8.99

TALES OF MYSTERY
Intermediate Level
00296769 6 Solos......................$8.99

LYNDA LYBECK-ROBINSON

ALASKA SKETCHES
Early Intermediate Level
00119637 8 Solos......................$8.99

AN AWESOME ADVENTURE
Late Elementary Level
00137563 8 Solos......................$7.99

FOR THE BIRDS
Early Intermediate/Intermediate Level
00237078 9 Solos......................$8.99

WHISPERING WOODS
Late Elementary Level
00275905 9 Solos......................$8.99

MONA REJINO

CIRCUS SUITE
Late Elementary Level
00296665 5 Solos......................$8.99

COLOR WHEEL
Early Intermediate Level
00201951 6 Solos......................$9.99

IMPRESIONES DE ESPAÑA
Intermediate Level
00337520 6 Solos......................$8.99

IMPRESSIONS OF NEW YORK
Intermediate Level
00364212......................$8.99

JUST FOR KIDS
Elementary Level
00296840 8 Solos......................$7.99

MERRY CHRISTMAS MEDLEYS
Intermediate Level
00296799 5 Solos......................$8.99

MINIATURES IN STYLE
Intermediate Level
00148088 6 Solos......................$8.99

PORTRAITS IN STYLE
Early Intermediate Level
00296507 6 Solos......................$8.99

EUGÉNIE ROCHEROLLE

CELEBRATION SUITE
Intermediate Level
00152724 3 Duets......................$8.99

ENCANTOS ESPAÑOLES (SPANISH DELIGHTS)
Intermediate Level
00125451 6 Solos......................$8.99

JAMBALAYA
Intermediate Level
00296654 2 Pianos, 8 Hands.....$12.99
00296725 2 Pianos, 4 Hands.......$7.95

JEROME KERN CLASSICS
Intermediate Level
00296577 10 Solos...................$12.99

LITTLE BLUES CONCERTO
Early Intermediate Level
00142801 2 Pianos, 4 Hands......$12.99

TOUR FOR TWO
Late Elementary Level
00296832 6 Duets......................$9.99

TREASURES
Late Elementary/Early Intermediate Level
00296924 7 Solos......................$8.99

JEREMY SISKIND

BIG APPLE JAZZ
Intermediate Level
00278209 8 Solos......................$8.99

MYTHS AND MONSTERS
Late Elementary/Early Intermediate Level
00148148 9 Solos......................$8.99

CHRISTOS TSITSAROS

DANCES FROM AROUND THE WORLD
Early Intermediate Level
00296688 7 Solos......................$8.99

FIVE SUMMER PIECES
Late Intermediate/Advanced Level
00361235 5 Solos...................$12.99

LYRIC BALLADS
Intermediate/Late Intermediate Level
00102404 6 Solos......................$8.99

POETIC MOMENTS
Intermediate Level
00296403 8 Solos......................$8.99

SEA DIARY
Early Intermediate Level
00253486 9 Solos......................$8.99

SONATINA HUMORESQUE
Late Intermediate Level
00296772 3 Movements.............$6.99

SONGS WITHOUT WORDS
Intermediate Level
00296506 9 Solos......................$9.99

THREE PRELUDES
Early Advanced Level
00130747 3 Solos......................$8.99

THROUGHOUT THE YEAR
Late Elementary Level
00296723 12 Duets....................$6.95

ADDITIONAL COLLECTIONS

AT THE LAKE
by Elvina Pearce
Elementary/Late Elementary Level
00131642 10 Solos and Duets.....$7.99

CHRISTMAS FOR TWO
by Dan Fox
Early Intermediate Level
00290069 13 Duets...................$8.99

CHRISTMAS JAZZ
by Mike Springer
Intermediate Level
00296525 6 Solos......................$8.99

COUNTY RAGTIME FESTIVAL
by Fred Kern
Intermediate Level
00296882 7 Solos......................$7.99

LITTLE JAZZERS
by Jennifer Watts
Elementary/Late Elementary Level
00154573 9 Solos......................$8.99

PLAY THE BLUES!
by Luann Carman
Early Intermediate Level
00296357 10 Solos....................$9.99

ROLLER COASTERS & RIDES
by Jennifer & Mike Watts
Intermediate Level
00131144 8 Duets......................$8.99

Prices, contents, and availability subject to change without notice.